To Todd, Mason and Samantha.
Your love inspires me and guides me.
You are my life and I love you with
every bit of my soul. -- L.F.

To Ma, Baba, & Onup
Thank you so much for your love
and support. -- S.R.

ISBN 978-0-9746526-7-2

Pixie's Food for Thought

Written by Lisa Fischer
Illustrated by Sanjida Rashid

My name is Samantha, my friends call me Pixie.

Dealing with allergies, that is the trick, see...

Sometimes I get rashes, sometimes I get hives.

My mom wrote this book to help save some lives.

2

My body doesn't like
to eat certain foods.

When I go out to eat, I need help to choose.

My body tries to fight the foods that I eat.

Like: Eggs, milk, peanuts and wheat.

I'm brave, strong and
know what to do.

If **someone** offers me food this may give you a clue.

Say "No thank you," be polite and walk away.

Don't be nervous, be proud and know what to say.

What's in that pasta, that bread or that bagel?

Ask a grown-up to tell you or just check the label.

I carry my EpiPen*
wherever I go.

I just use my imagination,
I wish it would glow.

*EpiPen is a federal registered trademark owned by Mylan Inc.

I am very special and
so are you.

There are lots of kids like us, that much is true!

Some kids are allergic to
dust, cats or dogs.

I even know someone who's allergic to frogs.

Everyone is different,
that's what makes us unique.

Make everyone listen to the words that you speak.

You sit at a special
table at school.

Allergy Table

This is of course because you're so cool!

No food allergy will ever
get me down.

Be sure to never hang your head low or frown.

Your body is beautiful,
inside and out.

Climb on the rooftops and give it a shout.

Always be aware of the foods that make you sick.

Awareness and knowledge, that is the trick.

Love your body and
don't feel blue.

I'm Pixie, I have allergies and this book is for YOU!

CPSIA information can be obtained
at www.ICGtesting.com
Printed in the USA
LVIC092134300712

292265LV00005B